HEI

Al _____ PUSHKIN

The Queen of Spades
and other stories

Translated from the Russian and retold by Stephen Colbourn

ROSS HIGH SCHOOL

TRANENT

HEINEMANN ELT   East Lothian Library Service

0580389

HEINEMANN ELT GUIDED READERS

INTERMEDIATE LEVEL

Series Editor: John Milne

The Heinemann ELT Guided Readers provide a choice of enjoyable reading material for learners of English. The series is published at five levels – Starter, Beginner, Elementary, Intermediate and Upper. At **Intermediate Level**, the control of content and language has the following main features:

Information Control

Information which is vital to the understanding of the story is presented in an easily assimilated manner and is repeated when necessary. Difficult allusion and metaphor are avoided and cultural backgrounds are made explicit.

Structure Control

Most of the structures used in the Readers will be familiar to students who have completed an elementary course of English. Other grammatical features may occur, but their use is made clear through context and reinforcement. This ensures that the reading, as well as being enjoyable, provides a continual learning situation for the students. Sentences are limited in most cases to a maximum of three clauses and within sentences there is a balanced use of adverbial and adjectival phrases. Great care is taken with pronoun reference.

Vocabulary Control

There is a basic vocabulary of approximately 1,600 words. Help is given to the students in the form of illustrations, which are closely related to the text.

Glossary

Some difficult words and phrases in this book are important for understanding the story. Some of these words are explained in the story, some are shown in the pictures, and others are marked with a number like this ...[3] Words with a number are explained in the Glossary on page 59.

Contents

Introductory Notes	4
The Queen of Spades	5
The Undertaker	18
The Postmaster	26
The Shot	34
The Blizzard	42
Points for Understanding	54
Glossary	59
List of titles at Intermediate Level	63

Introductory Notes

Aleksandr Pushkin (1799–1837)
Pushkin was the greatest Russian poet in the nineteenth century. He wrote many poems and several stories.

He spent most of his life in Saint Petersburg, the old capital of Russia. The rulers of Russia thought that Pushkin's writing was politically dangerous.

Pushkin was shot in a duel (see Glossary no 40) outside Saint Petersburg and died before his thirty-seventh birthday.

Note on Russian Names
In Russia, people do not use a form of Mr and Mrs together with a family name when they speak to each other. They use their first name and their father's name: for example, Pyotr Andreyevich (Pyotr the son of Andrey), Lizavyeta Ivanovna (Lizavyeta the daughter of Ivan). But friends and relatives use a short form of the first name when they speak to each other: for example, Marya becomes Masha and Avdotya becomes Dunya.

THE QUEEN OF SPADES

Hermann was a young man who lived in Saint Petersburg in Russia. His father had come from Germany to work in Russia before Hermann was born. When his father died, Hermann became an officer in the Russian army.

Hermann did not have much money. But many of the other officers had plenty of money. They loved to spend their evenings drinking wine and playing cards. Sometimes they stayed up all night gambling[1].

Hermann did not drink and did not play cards. He was very careful with his money, but he loved to watch the rich young men playing cards every night. He wanted to be rich, but he did not have enough money to gamble.

One of the young officers who gambled every night was called Tomsky. Tomsky often saw Hermann sitting at the card table and wondered why Hermann never played cards.

There was a party one night which went on until four o'clock in the morning. Tomsky lost a lot of money and was unhappy. He wanted someone to talk to, so he sat down beside Hermann.

'Why do you never play cards?' Tomsky asked Hermann.

'I have very little money,' Hermann replied. 'I cannot lose it at cards.'

'But you sit here every night and watch us win and lose,' Tomsky said.

'Yes,' Hermann agreed. 'I love cards very much.'

'So would you play cards if you were certain to win?'

5

The Queen of Spades

Tomsky asked with a smile.

'Perhaps,' Hermann answered slowly. 'But that's impossible.'

'Perhaps not,' said Tomsky. 'My grandmother, Countess[2] Anna Fedotovna, knows the secret of the Three Winning Cards. But she won't tell anyone and she never gambles.'

'I don't believe you,' said Hermann.

'Then listen to this story,' said Tomsky. 'My grandmother is more than eighty years old, but she was very beautiful when she was young.

'About sixty years ago, my grandmother went to Paris. She played cards with the Duke of Orleans and lost all my grandfather's money. My grandfather was very, very angry and said that he couldn't pay. He did not have enough money to pay the debt[3]. My grandmother was terribly worried and tried to borrow the money from a friend – a famous man called the Count Saint-Germain.

'The Count Saint-Germain was a mysterious person. He was extremely rich, but no one knew where the Count's money came from. He knew many strange secrets and he told my grandmother the secret of the Three Winning Cards. Perhaps Count Saint-Germain was in love with her, who knows?

'The next night, my grandmother played cards with the Duke of Orleans again. She played three cards – one after the other. They all won. She paid back the money and never gambled again. And she never told anyone the secret of the Three Winning Cards!'

'It can't be true,' said Hermann slowly. 'It's just a story, isn't it?'

'I don't think so,' said Tomsky. 'But look at the time! It's almost morning. It's quarter to six and time for bed.'

The Queen of Spades

All the young men finished their drinks and went home. It was nearly dawn on a cold winter morning.

Hermann could not stop thinking about Tomsky's story as he walked through the snowy streets of Saint Petersburg. If I knew the secret of the Three Winning Cards, I would be rich, he thought to himself. And if I was rich, I wouldn't waste[4] my money like Tomsky.

Hermann knew where Tomsky's grandmother lived and decided to walk past her big house. He stood on the opposite side of the street and looked up at the large windows of the house. In the early morning light, he saw a pretty young girl sitting at a window. Her face was sad, as if she had been crying. The girl looked down and saw Hermann staring at her. Hermann smiled and the girl's face turned red. She moved quickly away from the window. Hermann smiled thoughtfully to himself.

Later, he asked one of Tomsky's friends about the girl who lived in the old Countess's house.

'That's Lizavyeta Ivanovna,' the man replied. 'Her parents died when she was young and she went to live with the old Countess. But the Countess does not treat her well. Poor Lizavyeta lives in the house like an unpaid servant. She is not treated as a member of the family.'

Hermann made a plan to get into the old Countess's house. Every day he stood outside the big house and made sure that Lizavyeta saw him. After a week, he wrote her a letter.

The next morning, as Lizavyeta Ivanovna came out of the house with the old Countess, Hermann crossed the street towards them. While the servants were helping the Countess into her carriage, Hermann gave the letter to Lizavyeta and walked quickly away.

The Queen of Spades

Lizavyeta hid the letter. She read it later, when she was alone in her room.

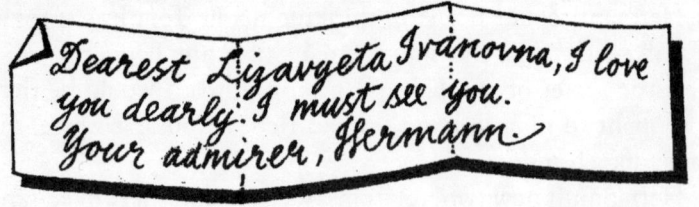

The poor girl did not know what to do. She lived like a prisoner in the big house. She had no friends. She had no one she could ask for advice.

She decided to write a note to Hermann and return his letter. The following day, when she saw Hermann in the street, she opened the window and threw the letter to him. Hermann picked it up and went away.

Lizavyeta's note said:

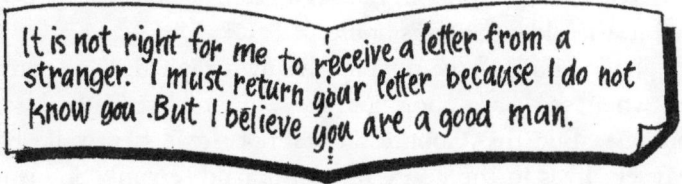

Hermann had expected Lizavyeta to answer in this way. For the next few days, he managed to give a letter to Lizavyeta every morning. She replied to his letters and her replies became longer and longer.

A week later, Lizavyeta threw the following letter out of the window:

The Countess will be at a ball tonight. She will not return until two o'clock in the morning. I will leave the front door unlocked. The servants will be asleep. Come at half past eleven. Go up the stairs and turn left. You will see the Countess's room in front of

8

'...she opened the window and threw the letter to him.'

The Queen of Spades

you. Go into the Countess's room. There are two doors behind a large, red curtain in her room. The door on the right leads to a small study, where nobody ever goes. Behind the other door, there is a staircase which leads up to my room.

Hermann waited impatiently all day. By ten o'clock that evening, he was outside the Countess's house. It was windy and snowing, but he felt neither the wind nor the snow.

Hermann watched the Countess get into her carriage and drive off. At exactly half past eleven, he entered the house. He ran up the stairs and went into the Countess's bedroom. The only light came from a golden lamp which burned in front of an icon[5].

Hermann did not go to Lizavyeta's room. Instead, he went through the door on the right, into the small study.

He stood in the darkness and silence, listening to all the clocks in the house strike twelve, then one, then two.

At last, a carriage drove up to the house. A few minutes later, servants carrying candles came into the bedroom, followed by the Countess.

Hermann watched from behind the red curtain. The servants dressed the old and ugly woman in her night clothes. But the Countess did not want to sleep. She sat in an armchair by the window and stared at the lamp. The servants blew out the candles and left her alone.

The Countess looked round as Hermann came out from behind the curtain.

'Don't be afraid,' Hermann said. 'I won't hurt you. I've come to ask you a question.'

The old woman was silent.

'You know the secret of the Three Winning Cards,' said Hermann. 'Tell me the secret and I will leave you in peace.'

10

The Queen of Spades

'No, no,' the Countess whispered. 'I can't tell you.'

'Why?' asked Hermann angrily. 'Don't you know the secret?'

The Countess said nothing.

'What use is the secret to you?' Hermann demanded. 'You are old. You don't need the money. You will die soon. Make me happy. Tell me the secret!'

The Countess said nothing.

The Queen of Spades

'You stupid old woman,' Hermann said. 'I will make you speak!' He took a pistol from his pocket.

The Countess raised her hands in front of her face, then fell back in the chair and did not move. Her eyes continued to stare at Hermann, but the eyes were lifeless. Hermann saw that she was dead.

He opened the door to Lizavyeta's room and walked up the stairs. Lizavyeta was still waiting for him. She was wearing her best dress. Her face was pale.

'Where have you been?' she whispered.

'In the old Countess's bedroom,' Hermann answered. 'The Countess is dead.'

Lizavyeta listened as Hermann told her how the Countess had died.

'I came here to find out a secret,' Hermann explained. 'I wanted to learn the secret of the Three Winning Cards. I asked the Countess to tell me. But she refused. Then suddenly, she fell back dead in her chair. I did not kill her.'

Lizavyeta's eyes filled with tears. She understood that his letters of love had meant nothing! She began to cry bitterly. She wanted to get Hermann out of the house as quickly as possible. She never wanted to see him again.

Lizavyeta dried her eyes.

'There is a secret staircase from the Countess's study,' she said. 'It leads down to a street behind the house. Here – take the key. Now go!'

Hermann left Lizavyeta's room and walked back down the staircase. He went back into the Countess's bedroom. The Countess's face was peaceful. Hermann was not sad that the Countess was dead. But he was sad that she had died without telling him her secret.

12

The Queen of Spades

Then he found the secret door in the study. He pushed it open and went down a dark staircase. The key unlocked a small door that led into the street. He walked out of the house and hurried away.

————

Three days later, Hermann went to the Countess's funeral[6]. The church was full. People went up one after the other to kiss the dead Countess's face as she lay in an open coffin[7]. Hermann followed them and went up to the coffin. He looked down at the dead Countess. Then suddenly, something strange happened. It seemed to Hermann that the dead woman opened one eye and winked[8] at him. Hermann stepped back in surprise, tripped over and fell to the stone floor. The people round the coffin helped Hermann to his feet and he hurried out of the church. At the same time, Lizavyeta Ivanovna fainted[9].

That afternoon, Hermann drank a lot of wine. He fell asleep on his bed without undressing. It was dark when he woke up. It was quarter to three in the morning. He thought that someone was looking in at the window. He sat up on the bed. A moment later, the door opened and a woman in a long white dress came in. It was the dead Countess!

'I have come to tell you my secret,' said the Countess. 'You must play only one card each night for three nights. Then you must never play cards again for the rest of your life. Also you must never tell anyone this secret. The Three, the Seven and the Ace will win for you.'

The Countess turned and went out of the door, closing it behind her. It was a long time before Hermann got up off his bed. He tried to open the door and found that it was locked.

————

13

The Queen of Spades

A famous gambler called Chekalinsky lived in Saint Petersburg. He had won millions of roubles[10] at cards and anyone was welcome to visit his house to play against him.

All the rich young men went to gamble at his table and Tomsky was a regular visitor. Hermann asked Tomsky to take him to Chekalinsky's house.

A game was being played when they arrived. Chekalinsky was dealing[11] the cards. Hermann waited for the game to end and then said, 'May I put down a card?'

Chekalinsky smiled and nodded. Hermann took a three from his pack of cards[12] and put it face down[13] on the table. Then he took his money out of his pockets and began to cover the card with money.

Chekalinsky was surprised. 'How much money do you want to bet?' he asked, staring at the pile of bank notes.

'Forty-seven thousand roubles,' Hermann answered.

Everybody turned and looked at Hermann.

'He's mad,' said Tomsky.

'He's drunk,' said another gambler.

'Excuse me,' said Chekalinsky, 'but that is a lot of money – far more than anyone has ever bet before.'

'Will you take the bet or not?' Hermann asked.

Chekalinsky nodded and began to deal the cards into two piles.

The cards on his right were the losing cards – the cards on his left were the winning cards. He turned over a nine to the right and on the left – a three.

'I win,' said Hermann, showing his card – a three. Chekalinsky smiled slowly, then counted out the money. Hermann took the money and left.

The Queen of Spades

The next evening, Hermann came back again to Chekalinsky's house. This time, he took a seven from his pack, put it face down on the table and covered it with all his money.

Chekalinsky started dealing. A jack turned up on the right and, to the left – a seven. Hermann showed his card. He had won again.

Chekalinsky's face was pale as he counted out ninety-four thousand roubles. Hermann put the money into his pockets and went out.

When Hermann appeared on the third evening, everyone was expecting him. Army generals and other important people had come to watch. They all stood in silence as Hermann sat down opposite Chekalinsky. Hermann put his card face down on the table. On top of his card, he put all his money – one hundred and eighty-eight thousand roubles.

Chekalinsky began dealing. His hands were trembling[14]. Then as he laid down the cards to his right and to his left, a queen fell on the right and an ace on the left.

'Ace wins!' cried Hermann and showed his card.

'Your queen has lost,' said Chekalinsky quietly.

Hermann looked again at the card in his hand. How had he made such a stupid mistake? Instead of an ace, he was holding the queen of spades!

As he looked at the card, the queen of spades seemed to open one eye and wink at him. She looked exactly like the dead Countess.

'The old woman!' Hermann shouted in horror.

But no one heard him. They were all cheering Chekalinsky. He was the winner.

'Well played!' shouted Tomsky.

15

Chekalinsky's face was pale as he counted out ninety-four thousand roubles.

The Queen of Spades

Nobody noticed Hermann as he turned round and walked out of the room in a daze[15]. No one in Saint Petersburg ever saw him again.

Hermann went mad and was put in a hospital. He spoke the same words over and over again. He never said anything else. 'Three! Seven! Ace! ... Three! Seven! Queen!!'

Lizavyeta Ivanovna married an army officer. They lived happily.

Tomsky married a princess.

THE UNDERTAKER

Adrian Prokhorov held a hammer in his right hand and a wooden board in his left hand. Between his teeth were four long nails. He climbed up onto a table outside the gates of his new house. He hammered the nails through the board and fixed it above the gates.

The noise of hammering brought several of his new neighbours out into the street. They stared up at the sign above Adrian Prokhorov's gates.

COFFINS FOR SALE – PLAIN AND COLOURED
OLD COFFINS REPAIRED
COFFINS FOR RENT

Adrian Prokhorov, the undertaker[16], was pleased with himself.

Business was good. Business was so good that he had bought a new house.

He was not usually a happy man. He lived with his two daughters and only spoke to them when he was angry or drunk. Then he shouted at them: 'Do this! Do that! Bring me this! Bring me that!'

Adrian was only happy when someone was dying. Then he put on his long, black kaftan[17] and his best black hat. As soon as the person was dead, he hurried to their house and offered to

18

The Undertaker

make all the funeral arrangements at a very reasonable price[18]. The relatives of the dead person did not usually argue about the cost. Adrian promised the best coffins, but did not always provide them. He made a lot of money in this dishonest way.

As he finished putting up the sign above his gates, he felt very happy. A rich widow[19], named Trukhina, was dying. Her funeral would be very expensive. Adrian Prokhorov expected her to die at any moment.

At that moment, a man dressed in a leather apron tapped Adrian on the shoulder. Adrian looked round. He hoped that the man was a messenger from the widow Trukhina's house.

'Good day,' said the man in the leather apron. 'My name is Gottlieb Schultz. I am a shoemaker and I live in the house opposite. I am your neighbour.'

Adrian Prokhorov did not like neighbours. He was also disappointed that the man was not a messenger from Trukhina's house. But Gottlieb Schultz spoke with such a funny German accent[20] that Adrian smiled.

Gottlieb Schultz thought that Adrian's smile was a friendly smile. 'Welcome new neighbour!' said Gottlieb warmly. He put his arms around Adrian's shoulders and kissed him three times.

'We are having a party tonight,' Gottlieb continued. 'It's our wedding anniversary[21]. My wife and I would like to invite you. Please do come.'

Adrian never invited anyone to his own house. But he did not refuse an invitation to a party if someone else was paying for it.

'Of course, of course,' he said. 'My daughters and I will be delighted to come.'

There followed an awkward silence. The two men did

*At that moment, a man dressed in a leather apron tapped
Adrian on the shoulder.*

The Undertaker

not know what to say to each other. After a pause, Adrian reluctantly[22] decided to invite the German into his house. 'Come in and have some tea,' he said. Then he shouted to his daughters, 'Girls! Bring the samovar[23] and two cups. And be quick about it!'

Gottlieb Schultz did most of the talking while they sat drinking tea. He talked about their businesses.

'But our two businesses – shoemaker and undertaker – are different,' said Adrian. 'The living can manage without shoes, but the dead cannot manage without coffins.'

Gottlieb laughed at this joke and got up from the table. 'So I'll see you this evening,' he said as he went out of the door.

Before going out that evening, Adrian Prokhorov spoke to the servant who worked in his kitchen. 'Remember,' he said to the girl, 'I'm expecting a messenger to come from the widow Trukhina's house. If a messenger comes to say that the widow is dead, you must tell me at once. You must run across the road to the shoemaker's house and tell me at once! At once! Do you hear?'

The shoemaker's house was crowded with guests. Most of them were German. There was plenty to eat and drink and soon everyone was enjoying themselves.

Gottlieb Schultz stood up and raised his glass. 'I drink a toast to the health[24] of my guests!' he shouted, and drank a glass of vodka. Other toasts were drunk – toasts to Moscow, toasts to Prussia, toasts to each other and toasts to their businesses.

Even Adrian Prokhorov looked happy after his tenth glass of vodka. 'You must all come to my housewarming[25] party,' he called out. But immediately he was angry with himself for

The Undertaker

giving such a stupid invitation. He hoped they would all forget about it.

Just before midnight, Gottlieb Schultz called for silence. 'Ladies and gentlemen,' he said, 'a final toast – a toast to the people we work for. To our customers!'

Everyone shouted back – 'To our customers!' – and emptied their glasses. They all laughed and cheered.

But Adrian Prokhorov did not drink a toast to the health of his customers. He did not want his customers to be healthy. People became his customers when they were dead. Also, Adrian was drunk. And when he was drunk he became angry.

'Take me home,' he ordered his daughters. They left the shoemaker's without saying goodbye and crossed the street to their house.

'They were laughing at me,' Adrian said to his daughters. 'They were laughing at me because I'm an undertaker. But they won't laugh at me when they need me.'

Adrian sat down heavily on his chair and tried to take off his boots. 'And I was going to invite them all to a housewarming! Oh, no, I won't do that. I'd rather invite my customers – the corpses[26] from their graves!'

'Don't say that, Father,' begged the two daughters. 'It's bad luck to speak of the dead. Let us take your boots off and put you to bed.'

'By God, I will invite my customers,' shouted Adrian. 'Do you hear me all you dead men? You're all invited to my house for a party!'

Just then, the church clock struck midnight. A horseman rode up to the gate with a message that the widow Trukhina was dead. Adrian Prokhorov put on his best black hat and rushed out of the house.

The Undertaker

He was away for an hour or two. When he had made all the arrangements for the burial, and agreed on a very high price with Trukhina's son, he returned home.

The gates of his house were open wide and so was the front door. There were people moving around inside the house.

'Who have my stupid daughters invited to my house at this time of night?' he asked himself angrily.

He stepped into the house. He was about to start shouting at the unwelcome guests. Then he stopped and almost fell over. The house was full of corpses! Their faces were blue and yellow and green in the candlelight. Their mouths hung open and their eyes were empty. There was a smell of something old and damp and rotten.

One of the corpses, dressed in the uniform of an army general, spoke to the undertaker in a horrible voice. 'You see, Prokhorov, we have accepted your invitation. Here are all the people you have buried.'

A small skeleton[27] pushed its way out of the crowd. Its fleshless bones were dressed in red rags. It rattled[28] as it walked and its skull seemed to smile a horrible smile.

'Don't you remember me, Prokhorov?' asked the skeleton in a terrible whisper. 'I'm Sergeant Pyotr Petrovich Kurilkin. I was your first customer. I was the first man you buried.'

The skeleton put out its arms to take hold of the undertaker and kiss him. Adrian Prokhorov cried out in horror and pushed the skeleton away. Pyotr Petrovich fell on the floor in a heap of bones.

The other corpses became angry. They all stretched out their bony hands and came towards the undertaker. He could not escape. He was surrounded. They grabbed his coat. They grabbed his hair. They scratched his face.

The house was full of corpses!

The Undertaker

Adrian Prokhorov screamed for help, then fell forward onto the bones of the dead sergeant, Pyotr Petrovich. Adrian struggled with the sheets that were wrapped round him like grave clothes.

'Father! Father! Wake up!' cried his daughters. 'You've fallen out of bed.'

'What happened? Where did they go?' asked the undertaker.

'Who?' said his elder daughter. 'You've been asleep all night, ever since we came back from the shoemaker's house.'

'And what about the widow Trukhina?' asked the undertaker. 'I must bury her today.'

'No, Father,' said the younger daughter. 'We have some good news. The whole town is talking about it. The widow Trukhina is well now. She isn't going to die.'

But it was not good news for Adrian Prokhorov. He was furious. 'Then let me go back to sleep again,' he said. 'I'd rather be with my customers in my dreams.'

THE POSTMASTER

I have travelled all over Russia. The weather is often bad. The roads are terrible. The coach drivers are stupid. And worse than all of these are the postmasters[29] – the men in charge of the posting stations.

The postmasters are usually rude. The horses are never ready on time. The posting stations are dirty and the postmasters charge too much money.

But I want to tell you a story about a good postmaster – a postmaster whom I liked. I only met him twice. The first time was in 1816, many years ago.

I was taking letters from Saint Petersburg to Kiev. The day was hot and the roads were dusty. But it began to rain before nightfall[30]. When I reached the posting station, my clothes were very wet and I was in a bad mood. I was ready to argue with the postmaster if he gave me any trouble.

However, the posting station was unusually clean and tidy. There were pictures on the walls and the samovar was boiling. I immediately felt more cheerful[31].

The postmaster appeared. 'Welcome, young sir,' he said cheerfully. He was a large man, with a friendly face. While I was changing into dry clothes, the postmaster called out, 'Dunya! Bring us some tea.'

A girl came from behind a curtain and poured tea. She was not more than fifteen years old, but she looked like a very beautiful woman.

26

The Postmaster

'Is this your daughter?' I asked the postmaster.

'Yes, sir,' he replied. 'Dunya is my daughter. She's clever and works hard. She reminds me more and more of her poor, dead mother.'

I talked to Dunya and she replied politely. All the time, she looked at me with her big blue eyes and smiled. She spoke like a young woman who had travelled in the world. But, of course, she had never left the country posting station. She had talked to travellers. She asked me questions about life in Saint Petersburg.

We became friends and, I must say, I took quite a fancy[32] to her. She knew my feelings, of course. She saw everything with those big blue eyes. She was much older and wiser than her fifteen years.

The horses were ready within an hour. I said goodbye to the postmaster and his daughter, Dunya. I wanted to stay longer, but my letters to Kiev were urgent.

Dunya followed me outside. Without her father seeing us, we kissed like lovers. The memory of those kisses is still clear in my mind today.

I did not return to that posting station for four years. But in 1820, I was travelling to Kiev and so I decided to visit Dunya and her father. Would they still be there? I wondered. Would they remember me? Would Dunya be married? How was the old postmaster?

I did not recognise the postmaster at first. He had changed completely and looked very old. He was dirty and untidy and so was the posting station.

I had a bottle of rum with me. I invited the old man to have a drink. 'How is your daughter, Dunya?' I asked gently, after we had drunk a glass or two.

The Postmaster

'God only knows,' replied the postmaster and as he drank the rum, he began to tell his sad story. 'In winter, three years ago, a young army officer stopped here,' said the postmaster. 'He was dressed in rich clothes and spoke like a lord. He demanded fresh horses for his troika[33]. When I told him there were no horses ready, he raised his whip to hit me.

'Dunya came in and saw what was happening. She was always clever. She smiled at the young man and offered him some food while he waited for his horses. He became quiet and polite. From that first moment, he couldn't stop looking at Dunya.

The Postmaster

'The horses were ready after supper. The young officer was preparing to leave when he suddenly fell over. He said he felt very ill and couldn't move. I put him in my bed and Dunya stayed by his side all night.

'The next day he was worse. I rode to the town to fetch a doctor. The doctor came and examined the officer. He said that the young man could not travel for a day or two. The officer paid him twenty-five roubles; which was far too much money. Later, I found out why he had paid the doctor so much money!

'On the following day, the officer was well again. It was a Sunday and Dunya was getting ready to go to church. The young man paid me well for the bed and his food. He offered to drive Dunya in his troika as far as the church.

'I was a fool! I let them go together. I should have guessed what was going to happen. Neither of them came back.'

The old man stopped speaking. There were tears in his eyes.

'And is that the last time you saw Dunya?' I asked gently.

'I'll tell you the rest of the story,' said the postmaster, pouring himself a drink. 'I found a man to look after the posting station while I was away. Then I set off, on foot, to follow my daughter and that worthless[34] officer.

'The first person I went to was the doctor who examined the officer. He told me that the officer had not been sick at all. The officer had paid him twenty-five roubles to tell a lie.

'I walked from one posting station to the next. At every posting station I asked about the officer. I knew his name from my register of travellers[35] – Captain Minsky!

'At last I arrived at Saint Petersburg. I stayed with an old army friend. I soon found out everything about Captain

The Postmaster

Minsky. He was known in the city. He was a gambler, a drinker and a womaniser[36]. He lived in rooms above a tavern.

'His servant let me in. Minsky recognised me at once. I begged him to give me back my daughter. He replied that Dunya was happy and did not want to return.

'He led me outside, holding my arm. He put something in my pocket and closed the door behind me.

'When I put my hand in my pocket, I found a hundred rouble banknote. I threw it on the pavement and walked away.

'After a moment, I thought it was foolish of me to throw the money away. I turned around, but I was too late. A well-dressed man picked up my hundred rouble note and put it in his pocket.

'I tried to see Minsky again, but his servant would not let me see him. I walked the streets of Saint Petersburg, day and night, not knowing what to do.

'One evening, I saw Minsky get out of a carriage and go into a large house. He was carrying a bunch of flowers.

'Was he visiting my daughter? I wondered. I thought quickly. There was an easy way to find out.

'I went up to the door and knocked. When a servant opened the door, I said I had an urgent message for Avdotya Samsonovna – my beloved Dunya.

'The servant said that I could not see Avdotya Samsonovna. She had a visitor and couldn't be disturbed. I pushed past her and entered the house. The rooms were in darkness but there was a light coming from under one door.

'I threw open the door and there was Minsky in the arms of a lady. A lady who was dressed in beautiful clothes and sparkling jewels. She was my Dunya!

The Postmaster

'Dunya looked at me, gave a terrible cry and fell to the floor. Minsky took hold of me and threw me into the street. That was the last time I saw them.

'What did you do?' I asked in a whisper.

The Postmaster

'What could I do?' said the old postmaster. 'I came back here to my job.'

'And don't you know what happened to Dunya?' I asked.

'No, I never saw her again after that night. But I think I know what happened to her.'

The old man's eyes filled with tears and he covered his face with his hands.

'I think Minsky grew tired of her. I think he put her out in the street like a broken toy – without money, without friends, with nowhere to go. That's what I think happened to her.

'Oh, Lord, have mercy on her. I often think of her walking the streets of that wicked city. How is she living? What if she has to sell her body for a few roubles? I wish she were dead rather than living such a life.'

I left the postmaster and went outside the posting house quietly. There was nothing I could do for him. The last time I saw him, he was on his knees in front of an icon, praying and weeping.

Many years passed, but I never forgot the sad story of the postmaster and his beautiful daughter. One autumn, I decided to visit the posting station again. I wanted to discover what had happened to the old man.

The sky was grey. A cold wind was blowing across the empty cornfields when I reached the posting station. Outside the door, where Dunya had kissed me, stood a fat woman. I asked if the old postmaster still lived there.

'No, sir, he died a year ago,' she replied.

'What did he die of?' I asked.

'Vodka, sir. He drank himself to death.'

'And where is the grave?'

The Postmaster

'In the graveyard, outside the village, sir,' answered the woman. 'My son will show you the way if you want.'

She shouted to a boy who was throwing stones at birds. 'Hey – Vanka! Show this gentleman where the old postmaster is buried.'

Vanka led me to the end of the village. I asked him if he had known the old man.

'Yes, sir,' answered Vanka. 'He was a kind old man. He used to give me nuts when he came out of the tavern. And he taught me how to whistle.'

The boy pointed. 'Here's his grave, sir,' said Vanka, standing on a mound of earth. 'You're not the first person I've brought here.'

'Who else has been here?' I asked in surprise.

'A beautiful lady, sir. She came in a coach with six white horses. And there were three children and a nurse[37] too.'

'And you brought her here?'

'She knew the way to the graveyard,' said Vanka. 'But she wanted someone to point out the grave. She stayed here a long time. Then she gave money to the priest to say prayers. And she gave me a silver five-kopek[38] coin.'

I, too, gave the boy a silver five-kopek coin and continued my journey. Now that I knew the end of the sad story, my own mind was at peace.

THE SHOT

When I was a young man, I was an officer in the army. We lived in a small town. Life was very boring. There were no girls. All the officers saw each other every day. We dined together, drank together and played cards together.

A stranger came to live in the small town. He was not an officer, but he had been in the army. He spoke and behaved like a Russian, but he had an Italian name – Silvio.

Silvio was a mysterious person. He had plenty of money to spend, but he dressed in old clothes and lived in a small house with two rooms.

Silvio often invited the army officers to dinner. The food was simple, but there was plenty of wine. We always went home drunk.

No one knew where Silvio came from and no one asked him. We were all a little afraid of Silvio.

He was about thirty-five years old, which, to us young men, seemed very old. Also, his hobby was shooting. He had a large collection of pistols. He was an excellent marksman[39] and he never missed the target.

We young men were very interested in duelling[40]. We often talked about duelling. I asked Silvio if he had ever fought a duel. He replied, simply, 'Yes', and said no more. I realised that he did not want to talk about it. Perhaps he had killed many men in duels.

A new officer arrived in the small town. We took him to meet Silvio, who invited us all to dinner. After dinner we played cards.

The Shot

We drank a lot of champagne. Everybody was drunk. The new officer made a mistake during the game of cards. Silvio pointed out the mistake to the officer who became angry.

'Are you accusing me of cheating[41], sir?' the officer shouted at Silvio.

There was anger burning in Silvio's eyes, but he said nothing. He stared at the officer in silence.

The officer picked up a bottle and threw it at Silvio's head. Silvio moved out of the way in time and the bottle smashed against the wall behind him.

'Please leave my house at once,' Silvio said to the officer slowly and coldly.

The Shot

We all thought that Silvio would challenge the officer to a duel. But several days passed and nothing happened. We were surprised. We were even more surprised when Silvio apologised to the officer. Was Silvio a coward[42]? Why had Silvio not challenged the officer to a duel?

I, alone, discovered Silvio's secret. The other officers never learnt the truth.

Friday was always a day of excitement. The mail coach[43] arrived, bringing letters, parcels and newspapers. Life was so boring that we read our letters to each other and felt sorry for the poor men who never received any mail.

Silvio never received any letters. But one Friday, a letter arrived for Silvio. It was from Saint Petersburg. I took it to him. He tore it open immediately and read it quickly.

'I must leave tonight,' Silvio said excitedly. 'I would like to say goodbye to all my friends. Please invite all the officers here for dinner at seven.'

We went to Silvio's house at seven. He had packed all his things in cases. After the meal, he said goodbye to each of us separately. Taking my hand, he said quietly, 'I want to speak to you when the others have gone.'

I waited for the other guests to leave. Then Silvio turned to me and said, 'I have always thought you are my friend. We may never meet again, so I want to tell you my story.'

'You remember the officer who threw the bottle at me?' Silvio began. 'You expected me to challenge that officer to a duel, didn't you? Perhaps you thought I was a coward. Let me explain. I cannot put my life in danger. Six years ago I was struck in the face by my worst enemy. That man is still alive. I have sworn[44] to kill him. That is why I must stay alive.'

'Is that why you are leaving now?' I asked.

The Shot

Silvio said nothing. He opened a case and took out an officer's cap. He put it on his head. I saw there was a bullet hole in it.

'I was an officer in the cavalry[45],' said Silvio. 'I was a young man and I was a great drinker and fighter. Duels took place every day. I never lost a duel. I was the best at everything.

'But a rich, young man from a famous family joined the cavalry. He was clever, good looking and brave. He was also a lucky gambler. All the ladies of Saint Petersburg liked him.

'Suddenly I was second best. This man was the best at everything. I hated him. I wanted to kill him.

'One night, we met at a dinner party. I wanted to make him angry. I was rude to him. He struck me in the face and challenged me to a duel. We agreed to fight with pistols outside the city early the next morning.

'I arrived before it was light. He was late. He walked up to me laughing. He was eating cherries which he had picked on the way. He looked young and handsome in the early morning light.

'We tossed a coin[46] to see who would shoot first. He won, of course. He was always lucky.

'We stood twelve paces apart. He raised his pistol and fired. The bullet went through my cap. He could have killed me easily, but he decided to miss.

'Then it was my turn. At a distance of twelve paces, it was impossible for me to miss. He knew that I could kill him easily. But he stood there, eating cherries, laughing at me. He was not afraid of death!

'But I could not shoot. I put down my pistol. I told him he would not see me again until the day of his death. I would choose that day carefully. I would visit him again when I knew he wanted to live. I would kill him then.'

'But he stood there, eating cherries, laughing at me.'

The Shot

Silvio was pale as he finished his story. He looked at me with burning eyes and I was afraid.

'And has that time now come?' I asked.

'Yes! It is his wedding night!' said Silvio.

We shook hands. I could not kiss Silvio goodbye. There was something frightening about him. One moment, he was as hot as fire. The next moment, he was as cold as ice.

Silvio got into his carriage and drove off. I never saw him again.

———

Five years later, my father died. I went to live on my estate[47] in the country. My neighbours were the Count and Countess Blagoy. They spent most of their time in Saint Petersburg.

One day, the Count and Countess visited their country estate. I decided to visit them and drove over to their great house.

A servant asked me to wait in the library. There were many fine books and paintings around the room. I noticed something unusual about one picture. I was looking at the picture when the Count and Countess came in.

'You are interested in my portrait[48],' said the Count.

'Yes, sir,' I replied. 'But why is there a bullet hole between the eyes?'

'It is not one hole, but two,' answered the Count. 'The second bullet passed through the hole made by the first.'

'A remarkable shot,' I said. 'I once knew a man who could shoot like that. He was the best marksman I have ever met.'

'And what was the name of this remarkable man?' asked the Count.

The Shot

'His name was Silvio,' I replied.

'Silvio!' said the Countess in surprise. Her face was pale. She sat down suddenly on a chair. The Count ran to her side and took her hand. 'I never want to hear that man's name again!' said the Countess.

'But we must give our guest an explanation,' said the Count. Then, turning to me, he said, 'We also knew Silvio.'

I suddenly realised that this was the man who had fought the duel with Silvio. 'Did Silvio promise to return and kill you?' I asked.

'Yes, he did,' replied the Count. 'Five years ago he stood where you are standing now.

'Five years ago, my wife and I were married. We came here for our honeymoon,' the Count continued. 'A servant told me that a man wanted to see me on business. When I came into the library, I found Silvio waiting for me. He had come to finish our duel.

'Silvio tossed a coin to see who would shoot first. I won, but I did not want to begin my marriage with murder. I fired the pistol above his head, between the eyes of my own portrait.

'Then it was Silvio's turn to shoot. But my wife heard the noise of the first shot. She came running into the library. She saw Silvio pointing his pistol at me and threw herself in front of me.

'Silvio stared at me for a long time. Then he turned and walked to the door. He had seen that I loved my wife. He had seen that I did not want to die. Then he did a strange thing. Before leaving, he pointed his pistol at my portrait. He fired his pistol and the bullet went between the eyes. His bullet passed

40

The Shot

through the hole made by mine. He left and we never saw him again.'

'Do you know what became of Silvio?' I asked.

'We heard that he was killed fighting in the war against the Turks. May God have mercy on him.'

THE BLIZZARD

This story begins in the year 1812. Marya Gavrilovna was a beautiful and happy young girl. She was seventeen years old and in love with an army officer.

She wrote long letters to the officer, whose name was Vladimir. And young Vladimir wrote long replies which he gave to Marya's maid.

The Blizzard

The two lovers met in a wood near Marya's house. But Marya Gavrilovna's parents found out about these meetings. They told their daughter that she must never meet the young man again. Marya was heartbroken[49]. But Vladimir still sent letters to her secretly.

Marya had read many French novels. In these love stories, often the lovers were separated by unkind parents. When that happened, the lovers ran away and got married secretly. So Marya decided to run away with Vladimir.

Vladimir said that he would find a priest to marry them. They would go to a church secretly. After they were married, they would go away for a few months. When they returned, he was sure that Marya's parents would forgive[50] them.

Marya agreed to Vladimir's plan. She told her maid what they were planning to do. The maid agreed to help them.

Marya and her maid planned to leave the house at night by the back door. Vladimir would send a sleigh[51] to meet them at the end of the garden. Then Vladimir's driver would take the two young women to the next village. Vladimir would be waiting for Marya at the church. There they would be married.

Marya packed her clothes in bags and her jewellery in a box. Then she wrote a letter to her parents asking them to forgive her. She went downstairs for supper. Her face was pale.

'What is the matter, Masha, my dearest?' her mother asked.

'Nothing, Mother,' Marya replied, trying to smile. 'I've got a headache and I'm not hungry. I think I'll go to bed.'

She kissed her mother goodnight and went upstairs. In her bedroom, she thought about leaving her home and her parents. She started to cry.

The Blizzard

Meanwhile, earlier that day, Vladimir had been to the village of Zhadrino. The priest in the church at Zhadrino had agreed to marry Vladimir and Marya.

Vladimir had also found two witnesses[52]. The village policeman and an old army officer agreed to be at Zhadrino church at half past nine that evening.

At eight o'clock, Vladimir sent his driver to fetch Marya and her maid. Vladimir then set off in a small sleigh for Zhadrino.

———

Marya and her maid left the house quietly at nine o'clock. The wind was blowing loudly. A blizzard[53] had started. The snow blew into their faces. They could not see the end of the garden. But they found the sleigh waiting for them.

Vladimir's driver was walking up and down to keep warm. He helped the girls into the sleigh with their bags. Then he drove into the blizzard towards the village of Zhadrino.

———

Vladimir drove through the thick snow. He could see nothing. The road had disappeared in the blizzard.

He drove on and on, but did not arrive at Zhadrino. He could not see Zhadrino. He could not see any houses at all. Vladimir was lost!

He reached a small wood. The trees gave him shelter from the wind. The snow was not so thick. Vladimir thought he knew where he was. But suddenly, the sleigh hit the root of a tree and overturned.

Vladimir was not hurt, but the sleigh was stuck in the snow. The wind blew stronger and the blizzard became worse.

The Blizzard

Vladimir could go no further. He found shelter for himself and his horses behind the sleigh and waited for the blizzard to stop. He fell asleep.

The first light of day woke him up. He was almost frozen,

45

The Blizzard

but he was able to push his sleigh the right way up. The blizzard had stopped and he could see smoke from the fires in Zhadrino in the distance.

The church of Zhadrino was locked. Vladimir went to the house of the priest to ask what had happened to Marya.

That morning, a doctor was called to the house of Marya Gavrilovna. Marya was in bed. She was very ill. For two weeks, her parents did not know if she would live or die.

All this time, Marya's mother sat beside her. Marya often talked in her sleep. Marya said the name of Vladimir over and over again.

Marya's mother decided that Marya was heartbroken because of her love for Vladimir. She spoke to her husband. They decided to write to Vladimir. They agreed to let him marry Marya.

But Vladimir had gone! After speaking to the priest at Zhadrino, Vladimir had returned to the army.

The priest at Zhadrino said nothing. He never told anybody what had happened that night. The two witnesses and Marya's maid said nothing. Marya's secret was safe. Her parents never knew that their daughter had left the house on the night of the blizzard.

In 1812, France attacked Russia. The French army marched towards Moscow. The French army was winning the war.

Marya and her family were far from the fighting. By

The Blizzard

summer, Marya was completely well. But she had become a quiet and thoughtful young woman. She no longer read French romantic novels and she did not laugh.

Bad news arrived in September. Vladimir had been wounded at the battle of Borodino. Marya fell sick again, but she recovered more quickly this time.

Worse news came. Vladimir died in Moscow when Napoleon's army captured the city. Marya's father also became ill and died before the end of the year.

Marya was now a beautiful and rich young woman. But she was very sad.

She went with her mother to live on their estate in the country. Marya had no friends and did not want to meet anybody.

When the French army captured Moscow, the Russians burnt the city. They did not want the French to have any food or shelter. The French army had to fight the Russian winter and lost. Napoleon took the French army back to France. The Russian army followed him. Hundreds of thousands of French soldiers died.

When the Russian soldiers came home, there were great celebrations. Many officers called at Marya Gavrilovna's house. She was polite, but cold.

However, she was attracted to one young officer named Burmin. He was the owner of a nearby estate. He had returned home from the fighting with medals for bravery. He was only twenty-six and was already a colonel. He was also very handsome. Burmin was not like the other officers. He was a quiet and serious man.

Marya and her mother invited Burmin to their house. Burmin began to visit them every day. Marya's mother asked

The Blizzard

her daughter if she was thinking of marriage. But Marya shook her head and looked thoughtful.

One day, Burmin arrived at the house and found Marya's mother sitting in the library. Burmin was wearing his best uniform and his medals.

'May I speak with your daughter alone?' Burmin asked.

'Of course, Colonel Burmin,' Marya's mother replied with a happy smile. 'She's in the garden.'

Marya Gavrilovna was reading a book. She looked up as Burmin walked across the garden.

Burmin stood in front of Marya, holding his cap in his hand. 'I have come ...' he began, 'to ask you to marry me, but ...'

'But,' Marya interrupted, 'I can never be your wife. There is another.'

'I know you loved another,' Burmin said. 'And I know that his death made you very sad. But, after three years, can you forget the past?'

Marya was silent. She did not look at Burmin.

Burmin looked sad. 'I have a terrible secret to tell you,' he said. 'I cannot ask you to marry me. I am not free. I am already married!'

Marya looked up in surprise.

'But please let me explain!' said Burmin. 'I do not know where my wife is, nor do I know her name.'

'What?' said Marya Gavrilovna. 'How very strange.'

'Please let me tell you my story,' Burmin said. 'Then you will understand.'

'Go on,' said Marya Gavrilovna patiently.

'It was early in the year 1812,' Burmin began. 'I was driving to Vilno and I was late. So I was in a great hurry.

The Blizzard

'The weather was bad. I had driven all night and all day without sleep. Then that evening, I was lucky to get a horse at a posting station. The postmaster told me to wait because a blizzard had started. But I decided to drive on.

'The blizzard became worse and I lost the road. The snow blinded me and I was very tired. I drank a lot of vodka to keep myself warm.

'Suddenly I saw a light and drove towards it. The light came from a village church. There were two or three sleighs outside. Someone shouted, "This way! This way!"

'I walked into the church not knowing where I was. There were a few candles burning. It was warm inside. So there I stood in my greatcoat, frozen and covered with snow, very tired and a little drunk. "Glory to God! You've arrived at last," someone said.

'A man took my arm and led me to a young woman dressed in a cloak. An old priest began the marriage service. I was happy to be a witness, but I thought it very strange. It seemed as if they had been waiting for me.

'The priest was in a hurry. Before I knew what was happening, I was married to the lady in the cloak. "Kiss one another!" said the priest.

'My new wife pulled back the hood of her cloak and turned to kiss me. I took off my cap.

'She stared at me in the candlelight. "It isn't him!" she cried and fell down onto the stone floor.

'The priest and the witnesses went to help the lady. I ran out of the church, jumped in my sleigh and drove off.'

'God have mercy on us!' cried Marya Gavrilovna. 'What happened to your poor wife?'

'I don't know what happened to her,' answered Burmin. 'I

The Blizzard

never knew the name of the village. Immediately afterwards, I had to go and fight Napoleon's army. We followed Napoleon all the way to Paris. I have no hope of finding the poor woman now.'

'Good God!' said Marya Gavrilovna, taking hold of his arm. 'So it was you! I was the woman you married in the church in Zhadrino.'

Burmin turned pale. He threw himself on the ground at Marya's feet.

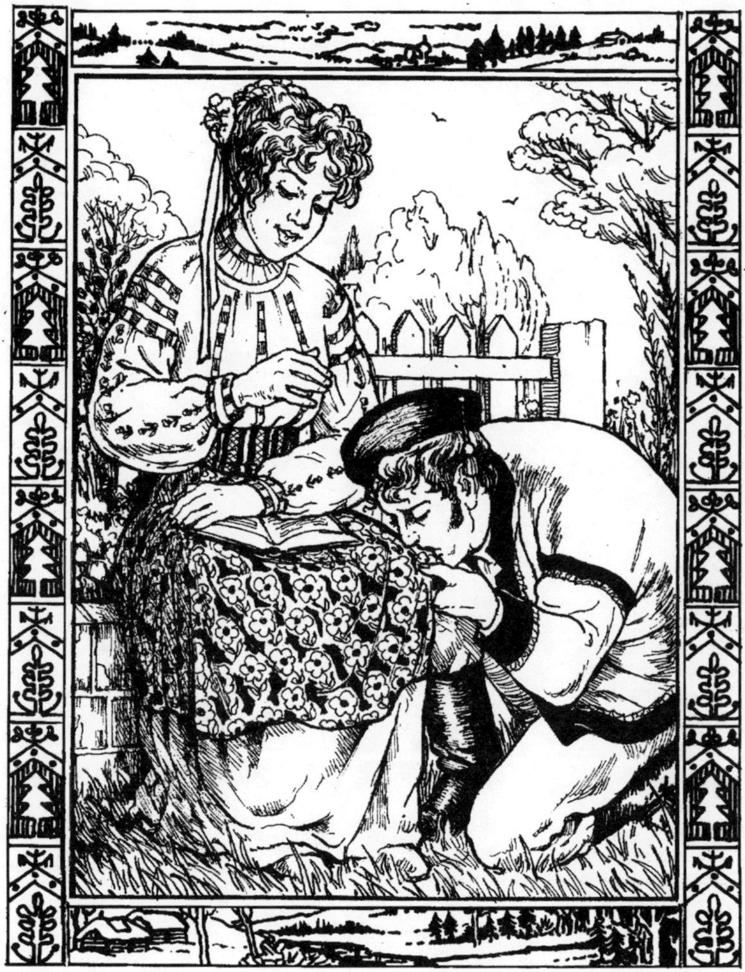

POINTS
FOR
UNDERSTANDING

ROSS HIGH SCHOOL
TRANENT

Points for Understanding

THE QUEEN OF SPADES

1 Why did Hermann not gamble?
2 Tomsky often saw Hermann sitting at the card table.
    (a) What did Tomsky do every night?
    (b) What did Tomsky wonder when he saw Hermann?
    (c) Why did Tomsky sit down beside Hermann?
3 'Why do you never play cards?' Tomsky asked Hermann.
    (a) What was Hermann's reply?
    (b) Would Hermann play cards if he was sure to win?
4 Tomsky told Hermann a story about the Countess Anna Fedotovna.
    (a) Who was the Countess Anna Fedotovna?
    (b) What secret did she know?
5 Why did the Countess Anna Fedotovna ask Count Saint-Germain for help?
6 How did Count Saint-Germain help her?
7 The Countess played cards again with the Duke of Orleans.
    (a) How many cards did she play?
    (b) What happened each time she played a card?
    (c) Did she ever gamble again?
8 What secret did the Countess never tell anyone?
9 What did Hermann think to himself after hearing this story?
10 Hermann made a plan to get into the old Countess's house.
    (a) Who was Lizavyeta?
    (b) How did Hermann make friends with Lizavyeta?
    (c) Why did Lizavyeta agree to let Hermann come into the Countess's house?
11 Where did Hermann hide inside the house?
12 How did the Countess Anna Fedotovna die?
13 Did she tell Hermann the secret before she died?
14 What happened when Hermann looked down at the Countess in her coffin?

15 The ghost of the dead Countess told Hermann the secret. What were the Three Winning Cards?
16 Hermann played cards with Chekalinsky. He won on the first two nights.
    (a) Why did Hermann think he had won on the third night?
    (b) Why did he lose?
17 Whose face did Hermann see on the Queen of Spades?
18 Why did Hermann go mad?

THE UNDERTAKER

1 What was Adrian Prokhorov's business?
2 Why had Adrian Prokhorov bought a new house?
3 Was Adrian Prokhorov usually a happy man?
4 Who did Adrian Prokhorov live with? Did he treat them kindly?
5 When was Adrian Prokhorov happy?
6 Why was Adrian Prokhorov waiting for a message from the house of the widow Trukhina?
7 Who was Gottlieb Schultz?
8 Why did he invite Adrian Prokhorov to his house?
9 Why did Adrian Prokhorov accept the invitation?
10 Why did Adrian Prokhorov not drink a toast to the health of his customers?
11 Adrian Prokhorov decided not to invite his neighbours to a housewarming party. Who did he invite instead?
12 Why did Adrian Prokhorov rush out of the house at midnight?
13 There was a party going on in Adrian Prokhorov's house when he got back.
    (a) Who were the guests?
    (b) Who was Sergeant Pyotr Petrovich Kurilkin?
14 Why was Adrian Prokhorov angry when his daughters woke him up?
15 Why did he want to go back to sleep?

THE POSTMASTER

1 Why did the storyteller not like posting stations?
2 What was different about the posting station on the road between Saint Petersburg and Kiev?

3 Who was Dunya?
4 Why did the storyteller take a fancy to Dunya?
5 When did the storyteller visit the posting station again?
6 What differences did the storyteller notice?
7 Why had the young officer paid the doctor a lot of money?
8 How had the young officer tricked the postmaster?
9 How did the postmaster know that the officer's name was Minsky?
10 Where did the postmaster go to find Minsky?
11 What did the postmaster learn about Minsky?
12 What happened when the postmaster met Minsky?
13 What happened when he met his daughter, Dunya?
14 What did the postmaster think had happened to his daughter?
15 Why did the storyteller go back to the posting station many years
   later?
16 Who showed him the postmaster's grave?
17 Who else had the boy taken to see the grave?
18 What had really happened to Dunya?

THE SHOT

1 Why was Silvio a mysterious person?
2 Why did no one know where he came from?
3 What was Silvio's hobby?
4 Why did the officers think that perhaps Silvio was a coward?
5 Why did Silvio want to fight with the rich young officer from a
   famous family.
6 Silvio fought a duel with the young officer.
    (a) Why had the young officer not killed Silvio?
    (b) Why did Silvio not kill the young officer?
    (c) When was Silvio going to kill him?
7 The storyteller went to live on his estate in the country.
    (a) Who were his neighbours?
    (b) Whose portrait did he notice on the wall?
    (c) What was strange about the portrait?
8 Why had Silvio not killed Count Blagoy?

56

THE BLIZZARD

1 Why was Marya heartbroken?
2 Why did Marya decide to run away with Vladimir?
3 What plans did Vladimir make?
4 Who had agreed to marry Marya and Vladimir?
5 Why did Vladimir not arrive at the church in Zhadrino?
6 Why did Marya's parents agree to write to Vladimir?
7 Why was Marya's secret safe?
8 What happened to Vladimir?
9 Why did Marya and her mother go to live on their country estate?
10 Who was Burmin? Why was he not like the other officers?
11 What was Burmin's terrible secret?
12 Who was Burmin's wife?

Glossary

1 **gamble** (page 5)
to play cards hoping to win money. A gambler plays cards or other games hoping to win money. The card game in "The Queen of Spades" is called *faro*. This is a simple game. Players choose a card from their own packs and bet money. The dealer then deals a pack of fifty-two cards into two piles. The cards on the right lose and the cards on the left win. The suits in a pack of cards are: hearts, clubs, diamonds, spades. The highest cards in each suit are: Jack, Queen, King, Ace.

2 **Countess** (page 6)
in Russia titles were given to rich landowners and members of the royal family. Other titles used in this story are Count and Duke.

3 **debt** (page 6)
money which must be paid to someone.

4 **waste** (page 7)
to spend money foolishly.

5 **icon** (page 10)
a religious painting.

6 **funeral** (page 13)
the burial of a dead person which begins with a service in church.

7 **coffin** (page 13)
a wooden box in which the body of a dead person is put before the body is buried in the ground.

8 **winked** (page 13)
to wink is to look at a person and shut one eye quickly. You give someone a wink to show that there is a secret known to you and the other person.

9 **fainted** (page 13)
to fall down suddenly because you do not feel well.

10 **roubles** (page 14)
Russian money.

11 **dealing** (page 14)
to deal cards is to put them on the table at the beginning of each game.

12 **pack of cards** (page 14)
there are fifty-two cards in a pack of cards.

13 **face down** (page 14)
   to put a card down on the table so that no one can see which card it is.

14 **tremble** (page 15)
   to tremble is to shake. Chekalinsky's hands were shaking.

15 **daze** – *in a daze* (page 17)
   when someone is in a daze, they cannot see or hear clearly. They do not know what is happening round them.

16 **undertaker** (page 18)
   a man who makes coffins and arranges funerals.

17 **kaftan** (page 18)
   a long shirt with a belt, worn by Russians.

18 **price** – *at a reasonable price* (page 19)
   as cheaply as possible.

19 **widow** (page 19)
   a woman whose husband is dead.

20 **German accent** (page 19)
   the way the shoemaker spoke Russian showed that he had been born in Germany. He spoke Russian with a German accent which sounded funny.

21 **anniversary** – *wedding anniversary* (page 19)
   an anniversary is a day on which something important happened on the same date in the past. A wedding anniversary is the day on which a couple were once married. Usually, there is a party on the day of a wedding anniversary.

22 **reluctantly** (page 21)
   to do something without really wanting to.

23 **samovar** (page 21)
   a tall, metal pot used in Russia for boiling water to make tea.

24 **health** – drink a toast to the health (page 21)
   to drink a toast to the health of someone is to stand up with a full glass in your hand and wish them good health. Then you drink what is in the glass.

25 **housewarming** (page 21)
   a party which people give when they move into a new house. They usually invite their friends and neighbours to the housewarming party.

26 **corpse** (page 22)
   the body of a person who has died.

27 **skeleton** (page 23)
the bones of a dead body.

28 **rattle** (page 23)
to rattle is to make a sharp noise. Here it is the noise made by the bones of the skeleton knocking together.

29 **postmaster** (page 26)
in the nineteenth century, people travelled in coaches pulled by horses. The coaches often carried post – letters and parcels – and the coaches stopped at Posting Stations. At the Posting Stations the passengers could rest and eat meals. The tired horses could rest and more horses could take the coach on the next part of the journey.

30 **nightfall** (page 26)
the time when the sun goes down and it gets dark.

31 **cheerful** (page26)
happy.

32 **fancy** – *take a fancy to someone* (page 27)
to like someone from the first moment you see them.

33 **troika** (page 28)
an open coach pulled by three horses.

34 **worthless** (page 29)
a worthless person is a bad person.

35 **travellers** – *register of travellers* (page 29)
when someone is travelling on a journey and stays in a hotel, they must write their name and address in a book. This book is called the register.

36 **womaniser** (page 30)
a man who loves many women.

37 **nurse** (page 33)
a woman who works for a rich family. Her job is to take care of the young children.

38 **kopek** (page 33)
Russian money. One rouble was equal to one hundred kopeks.

39 **marksman** (page 34)
someone who is able to aim a gun at a target and hit it. The target can be a person or an animal.

40 *duelling* (page 34)

at one time, duelling was popular in Europe among gentlemen and army officers. A duel was a fight in which the men fought with either pistols or swords. The people taking part in a duel followed agreed rules.

41 *cheating* (page 35)

to cheat at cards is to play dishonestly.

42 *coward* (page 36)

a person who is not brave.

43 *mail coach* (page 36)

a coach pulled by horses which took letters and parcels to towns and villages.

44 *sworn* (page 36)

to swear to do something is to make a promise to God to do it.

45 *cavalry* (page 37)

soldiers who fought on horses.

46 *coin – to toss a coin* (page 37)

to make a decision by throwing a coin up in the air. The decision is made by the way the coin falls on the ground.

47 *estate* (page 39)

the land owned by a rich family in the country.

48 *portrait* (page 39)

a painting of a person which shows the person's face clearly.

49 *heartbroken* (page 43)

feeling very sad and unhappy.

50 *forgive* (page 43)

when you are no longer angry with someone because they have done something wrong, you forgive them.

51 *sleigh* (page 43)

a carriage without wheels which is used for going over snow.

52 *witnesses* (page 44)

the witnesses at a wedding are two people who sign a book to say that the wedding took place.

53 *blizzard* (page 44)

a snow storm. In a blizzard, the snow falls so thickly that no one can see where they are going.

A SELECTION OF GUIDED READERS AVAILABLE AT

INTERMEDIATE LEVEL

Shane *by Jack Schaefer*
Old Mali and the Boy *by D. R. Sherman*
Bristol Murder *by Philip Prowse*
Tales of Goha *by Leslie Caplan*
The Smuggler *by Piers Plowright*
The Pearl *by John Steinbeck*
Things Fall Apart *by Chinua Achebe*
The Woman Who Disappeared *by Philip Prowse*
The Moon is Down *by John Steinbeck*
A Town Like Alice *by Nevil Shute*
The Queen of Death *by John Milne*
Walkabout *by James Vance Marshall*
Meet Me in Istanbul *by Richard Chisholm*
The Great Gatsby *by F. Scott Fitzgerald*
The Space Invaders *by Geoffrey Matthews*
My Cousin Rachel *by Daphne du Maurier*
I'm the King of the Castle *by Susan Hill*
Dracula *by Bram Stoker*
The Sign of Four *by Sir Arthur Conan Doyle*
The Speckled Band and Other Stories *by Sir Arthur Conan Doyle*
The Eye of the Tiger *by Wilbur Smith*
The Queen of Spades and Other Stories *by Aleksandr Pushkin*
The Diamond Hunters *by Wilbur Smith*
When Rain Clouds Gather *by Bessie Head*
Banker *by Dick Francis*
No Longer at Ease *by Chinua Achebe*
The Franchise Affair *by Josephine Tey*
The Case of the Lonely Lady *by John Milne*

For further information on the full selection of
Readers at all five levels in the series, please refer
to the Heinemann ELT Readers catalogue.

Macmillan Heinemann English Language Teaching, Oxford

A division of Macmillan Publishers Limited

Companies and representatives throughout the world

ISBN 0 435 27239 X

Heinemann is a registered trademark of Reed Educational & Professional Publishing Limited

This retold version for Heinemann ELT Guided Readers
© Stephen Colborn 1988, 1922
First published 1988
Reprinted twice
This edition published 1992

All rights reserved; no part of this publication may be
reproduced, stored in a retrieval system, or transmitted, in any
form or by any means, electronic, mechanical, photocopying,
recording or otherwise, without the prior written permission of
the Publishers.

Illustrated by Kay Dixey
Typography by Adrian Hodgkins
Cover by Paul Wearing and Threefold Design
Typeset in 11/13.5 pt Goudy
by Joshua Associates Ltd, Oxford
Printed and bound in Spain by Mateu Cromo S.A.

99 00 01 02 7 6 5 4